A Story a Day 'til Christmas

VOLUME III

It is good to be children sometimes,
and never better than at Christmas,
when its mighty Founder was a child Himself.

❧

CHARLES DICKENS

EDITED BY JONNA GRESS AND NAN ROLOFF

Current

Library of Congress Catalog Card Number:
91-77679

ISBN 0-944943-05-5

Contents

Sunshine and the Very First Christmas

BY ANDREA DORAY • ILLUSTRATED BY SHARON SANDNER CARTWRIGHT

A long time ago, before the first Christmas, there was a donkey named Sunshine.

Sunshine lived with Joseph and Mary in a village called Nazareth. Sunshine was such a part of the family that Mary and Joseph would often stop to pet and talk to him.

But Sunshine was not happy.

Joseph and Mary were very poor. Mary worked in the house, preparing meals and weaving cloth. Joseph was a carpenter, and he was very busy, too. He often took Sunshine with him to get wood to make tables and chairs and beds for the people in Nazareth.

Sometimes, Joseph and Sunshine would deliver what Joseph had made to the people in the village. Sunshine had many donkey friends and, at first, he liked going with Joseph.

But then his donkey friends began to tease him. "Sunshine, you don't have a blanket," they said. Some of the other donkeys had blue blankets, some had red blankets, and one even had a blanket with all the colors of the rainbow.

The other donkeys weren't very nice. They paraded in front of him with their fancy blankets. "Why don't you have a blanket?" they asked him. "Is your family too poor for one?" Sunshine was ashamed. Sometimes, he wished he belonged to another family.

Every time he went with Joseph to the village, he would hang his head. Mary and Joseph saw that Sunshine was sad, but they had other things to think about, too. Mary was going to have a baby!

Then, one day, Joseph came to get Sunshine. Joseph was very excited. "We're going to Bethlehem," he said to the donkey. "It will be a long journey. I will walk, but Mary must ride because she is going to have her baby soon."

Sunshine stood very still while Joseph tied bundles and baskets to his sides. All he could think about was wanting a new blanket. When they were ready to leave, Joseph asked, "Sunshine, why are you so sad?"

Then Mary said, "I know what will make Sunshine happy." Out of the bundles, she took a beautiful blanket which she placed on Sunshine's back. "I made this for the baby, but now it's yours," she said.

Sunshine was so proud! He remembered how all the other donkeys had teased him, and he called to them as he left the village, "See my new blanket! My blanket is the best one of all!"

The journey was long and hard. When they finally reached Bethlehem, Mary and Joseph were very tired. Joseph told Mary, "We must find a place for the night." They stopped at the inn and asked for somewhere to stay because Mary was ready to have her baby.

The innkeeper said the inn was full, but Joseph and Mary could stay in the stable. So, they went down to the stable and Joseph talked softly to the cows and the lambs and the camels that lived there. He gathered some fresh hay to make a bed for Mary. Joseph made room for Sunshine, fed him, and took off the beautiful new blanket for the night.

During the night the miracle of the first Christmas happened! The baby Jesus was born right there in the stable with Sunshine and the other animals! Mary used a manger filled with sweet hay as a crib, but she had nothing to cover the baby.

The other animals said, "Sunshine! Why don't you give your new blanket to the baby?" But Sunshine didn't want to give up his new blanket.

He remembered how the donkeys in Nazareth teased him. Wasn't it his blanket? Wouldn't all the other animals laugh at him if he didn't have one?

"Sunshine, think how lucky you are!" the wise old camel said. "You have a family that loves you and takes care of you. They feed you and give you shelter. You even have a brand new blanket!"

"Sometimes, though," the camel said, "it's not important what you have, but what you do to help others."

"I gave my stall to the baby Jesus," said the cow. "We gave our manger to the baby Jesus," said the lambs. "And I gave all my hay to the baby Jesus," said the camel. Sunshine saw how happy all these animals were. No one was laughing at them for sharing what they had.

"Maybe being part of a family means more than just having the things I want," thought Sunshine. "Families need to take care of each other."

He took his beautiful blanket and gave it to Mary to cover the baby.

The other animals cheered! "Sunshine, you have given a wonderful gift!" the wise old camel said. "You have showed that the true meaning of Christmas will always be helping others without thinking of yourself."

Mary wrapped the baby Jesus in the beautiful blanket. Joseph hugged Sunshine, and brushed him, and put clean hay in his stall. And Sunshine was the happiest donkey of all on that very first Christmas.

The Legend of Babouschka

BY CHERIE RAYBURN • ILLUSTRATED BY CARY HEATH

Along time ago in Russia, there was an old woman named Babouschka. She lived in a little hut in the coldest corner of that cold, cold country. Here the winter wind rattled loudly at her windows and piled deep snow drifts around her cozy little house. And though Babouschka lived where four roads met, in the months when the snow flew, not one person ever passed by her door.

But one winter night, in the gloomy dusk, a most strange thing happened. Babouschka heard, far away, the tink, tink, tinkling of bells and the sound of voices. She peered out of her frost-laced window. Down the widest of the snow-covered roads, she could see a large procession of people.

As they drew closer, she caught her breath at the sight of three men astride camels. Indeed, these were kings, Babouschka thought. They wore magnificent crowns, the jewels of which gleamed in the fading light. Their heavy fur wraps looked thick and warm, and they were attended by many servants.

Babouschka caught her breath again—they were stopping at her house! There was a knock at her door. What could such persons want of her, she wondered. As she opened the door, the howling wind and swirling snow rushed inside her warm home.

One of the kings said, "We are on a long journey, for we have seen a wondrous star in the sky. It shines over a town where a newborn baby lies, and it is for Him that we search. But now the star is hidden behind the clouds. Can you at least tell us the way to the next village?"

"Who is this child?"

"A king, and we go to worship Him. Come with us, Babouschka. Such a child there has never been."

Babouschka peered into the dark, cheerless night. She felt the warmth of her home at her back. The star was nowhere to be seen, and, as the bitter wind howled again, she shook her head no. "I cannot go. Not now," she said. "Perhaps tomorrow."

But the kings could not wait for her. By the next morning, they were far ahead on their journey, and even the tracks of the camels had been swept beneath the deep snow.

As the days passed, poor Babouschka thought a great deal about the kings, of their glory, and their vision of the little baby. The more she thought, the more her heart hurt. Ah, she sighed, if only she had gone with them!

Day by day, her regret grew over the chance she had missed. The child became her first and only thought. One day, she could stand it no longer. She wrapped herself in her warmest shawl, filled her basket with her best belongings, and shut the door of her house behind her.

Babouschka had no hope of overtaking the three kings. But she thought she might find the Child they had sought, so that she, too, might love and worship Him. And so her journey began.

It is said in Russia that it still continues, that all through the winter months Babouschka walks through fields and villages searching for the Holy Child. In the late nights, when tired mothers sleep, she tiptoes into nurseries and peeks beneath the blankets that cover the sleeping children, hoping to discover the Holy Child there. Then she gently lays the coverlet down and slips away in silence. And always she leaves behind a candy or trinket, something she hopes will lighten the heart of the little child she has left.

When children in Russia awaken at Christmastime to find candy and toys, they know that Babouschka has been there—and that she is still searching for the Holy Child.

The Greatest Story Ever Told

FROM THE LIVING BIBLE
LUKE 2:1–20
ILLUSTRATED BY MARK MUELLER

Caesar Augustus, the Roman Emperor, decreed that a census should be taken throughout the nation. Everyone was required to return to his ancestral home for this registration. And because Joseph was a member of the royal line, he had to go to Bethlehem in Judea, King David's ancient home—journeying there from the Galilean village of Nazareth. He took with him Mary, his fiancee, who was obviously pregnant by this time.

And while they were there, the time came for her baby to be born; and she gave birth to her first child, a son. She wrapped him in a blanket and laid him in a manger, because there was no room for them in the village inn.

That night some shepherds were in the fields outside the village, guarding their flocks of sheep. Suddenly, an angel appeared among them, and the landscape shone bright with the glory of the Lord. They were badly frightened, but the angel reassured them.

"Don't be afraid!" he said. "I bring you the most joyful news ever announced, and it is for everyone! The Savior—yes, the Messiah, the Lord—has been born tonight in Bethlehem! How will you recognize him? You will find a baby wrapped in a blanket, lying in a manger!"

Suddenly, the angel was joined by a vast host of others—the armies of heaven—praising God: "Glory to God in the highest heaven," they sang, "and peace on earth for all those pleasing him."

When this great army of angels had returned again to heaven, the shepherds said to each other, "Come on! Let's go to Bethlehem! Let's see this wonderful thing that has happened, which the Lord has told us about."

They ran to the village and found their way to Mary and Joseph. And there was the baby, lying in the manger. The shepherds told everyone what had happened and what the angel had said to them about this child. All who heard the shepherds' story expressed astonishment, but Mary quietly treasured these things in her heart and often thought about them.

Then the shepherds went back again to their fields and flocks, praising God for the visit of the angels, and because they had seen the child, just as the angel had told them.

The Birds' Christmas Carol

BY KATE DOUGLAS WIGGIN • ILLUSTRATED BY CLAUDIA HEASTON

It was very early Christmas morning, and in the stillness of the dawn, with the soft snow falling on the housetops, a little child was born in the Bird household. They had intended to name the baby Lucy, if it were a girl; but they had not expected her on Christmas morning, and a real Christmas baby was not to be lightly named—the whole family agreed on that.

They were consulting about it in the nursery. Mr. Bird said he had assisted in naming the three boys, and he should leave this matter entirely to Mrs. Bird. Donald wanted the child called Dorothy, after a pretty, curly haired girl who sat next to him in school. Paul chose Luella, for Luella was the nurse who had been with him during his whole babyhood, up to the time of his first trousers, and the name suggested all sorts of comfortable things. Uncle Jack said the first girl should always be named for her mother, no matter how hideous the name happened to be.

Grandma said she would prefer not to take any part in the discussion, and everybody suddenly remembered Mrs. Bird had thought of naming the baby Lucy, for Grandma herself; and, while it would be indelicate for her to favor that name, it would be against human nature for her to suggest any other, under the circumstances.

Hugh, up until now the baby of the family, sat in one corner and said nothing, but felt in some mysterious way that his nose was out of joint; for there was a newer baby now, a possibility that he had never taken into consideration;—and the "first girl," too—which made him positively green with jealousy.

The reason the subject had been brought up at all so early in the day lay in the fact that Mrs. Bird never allowed her babies to go overnight unnamed. She said that to let blessed babies go dangling and dawdling about without names for months and months was enough to ruin them for life.

So Donald took his new scooter and went out to ride it up and down the stone pavement, while Paul spun his musical top on the front steps.

But Hugh refused to leave the scene of action. He seated himself on the top stair in the hall and subsided into gloomy silence, waiting to declare war if any more "first girl babies" were thrust upon his family.

Meanwhile, dear Mrs. Bird lay in her room, weak, but safe and happy, with her sweet baby girl by her side. Nurse was making breakfast in the kitchen, and the room was dim and quiet. There was a cheerful fire in the grate, but though the shutters were closed, the side windows that looked out on the little church next door were open a little.

Suddenly, a sound of music poured out into the bright air and drifted into the chamber. It was the boys' choir singing Christmas anthems. Their clear, fresh voices, full of hope and cheer, rose higher and higher, singing in joyful harmony:

> *Carol, brother, carol,*
> *Carol joyfully,*
> *Carol the good tidings,*
> *Carol merrily!*
> *And pray a gladsome Christmas*
> *For all your fellow-men:*
> *Carol, brother, carol,*
> *Christmas Day again.*

One verse followed another, always with the same sweet refrain:

> *And pray a gladsome Christmas*
> *For all your fellow-men:*
> *Carol, brother, carol,*
> *Christmas Day again.*

Mrs. Bird thought, as the music floated in upon her gentle sleep, she had slipped into heaven with her new baby, and the angels were bidding them welcome. But the tiny bundle by her side stirred a little, and Mrs. Bird opened her eyes and drew the baby closer. Her baby looked like a rose dipped in milk, she thought, like a pink cherub with its halo of pale yellow hair...

> *Carol, brother, carol,*
> *Carol joyfully,*
> *Carol the good tidings,*
> *Carol merrily!*

The voices were brimming over with joy.

"Why, my baby," whispered Mrs. Bird in soft surprise, "I had forgotten what day it was. You are a little Christmas child, and we will name you Carol—Mother's Christmas Carol!"

"What!" said Mr. Bird, coming in softly and closing the door behind him.

"Why, Donald, don't you think Carol is a sweet name for a Christmas baby? It came to me just a moment ago in the singing, as I was lying here half asleep and half awake."

"I think it is a charming name, dear heart, and sounds just like you, and I hope that, being a girl, this baby is as lovely as her mother," Mr. Bird said, causing Mrs. Bird to blush with happiness.

And so Carol came by her name.

Perhaps because she was born at Christmastime, Carol was a very happy baby. Of course, she was too tiny to understand the joy of Christmas, but people say there is everything in a good beginning, and she may have breathed in the fragrance of evergreens and holiday dinners, while the peals of sleighbells and the laughter of happy children may have fallen upon her baby ears.

Her cheeks and lips were as red as holly berries. Her hair was the color of a Christmas candle flame. Her eyes were as bright as stars. Her laugh like a chime of Christmas bells. Her tiny hands forever outstretched in giving.

Such a generous little creature you ever saw. A spoonful of bread and milk had always to be taken by Mamma or Nurse before Carol could enjoy her supper. Whatever bit of cake found its way into her pretty fingers was broken in half to be shared with Donald, Paul, or Hugh. When they pretended to nibble the morsel with affected enjoyment, she would clap her hands with delight.

"Why does she always share so joyfully?" asked Donald thoughtfully. "None of us boys ever did."

"I don't know," said Mamma, holding her darling Carol to her heart, "except that she is a little Christmas child and has a tiny share of the most blessed birthday the world ever knew!"

Angie's Heavenly Journey

BY NANCY BRUMMETT
ILLUSTRATED BY CONNIE BECK

Angie Angel had never even seen an angel until she went to heaven and became one. Why, the closest she had ever come to seeing an angel was the time she saw an angel fish in a tidal pool! Now she was in heaven, assigned to the Music Cloud to work on polishing and tuning the harps. Angie knew even less about harps than about angels. And there were so many of them!

One day Angie was given more harps to polish and tune than usual. All the Heavenly Host were in a flurry of excitement at the news that the Christ Child would soon be born in Bethlehem. The rehearsal schedule for the Celestial Choir had been doubled and the Choirmaster insisted that every trumpet and harp be kept in perfect condition.

Angie didn't mind the extra work. She just thought about how wonderful it would be when the Baby was born. It would be a birthday party like no other! Whenever she had time, Angie practiced playing the harp herself. Maybe, just maybe, she could play for the Christ Child, too!

Of all the harps in heaven, Angie's favorite was the one that had belonged to King David. As a child on Earth, Angie had heard many stories about how bravely David had killed the evil giant, Goliath, with his slingshot, when he was just a boy. When David grew up to be a king, he wrote beautiful poetry and, playing the harp Angie adored, sang the Psalms that are now recorded in the Holy Bible.

"Oh, it's so beautiful," Angie thought, as she gazed at King David's harp in the glass case where it was carefully stored. "I bet the Christ Child will hear its pure melody above all the others and be so very pleased."

There was much excitement in heaven now, as the heavenly word was that the Baby could be born any minute! Finally, one day Angie got up the courage to ask the Celestial Choirmaster if she could go to celebrate the Christ Child's birth, too.

"Uhh…excuse me, sir," Angie said in a very small voice.

"Yes, child, what is it? Can't you see I'm busy here?"

"I'm sorry to bother you, sir, but I only thought… that is, I was just wondering…"

"Yes, yes, what is it? What is it?" the Choirmaster snapped.

"I want to know if I can go play for the Christ Child, too. I won't be any trouble at all. I promise!"

"Heavens, child, of course not. You really aren't a very good musician and you could never make such a long, difficult flight carrying a harp. No, I'm afraid it is out of the question. Besides, you're needed here."

Angie knew there was no sense in arguing. She was so sad she didn't feel like sliding down the golden banisters or stopping to talk to St. Peter at the pearly gates. She just slowly walked back to her own little cloud to snuggle in for the night. A tear trickled down her cherub cheek and onto the cloud pillow beneath her head. As she closed her eyes, she prayed she would dream of the Christ Child.

The next morning, when Angie awoke, everything seemed strangely quiet. The heavenly peace seemed even more peaceful than usual. As she rushed to the Music Cloud to begin her day's work polishing harps, she passed St. Peter.

"What's happened?" Angie asked the kind old gentleman. "Where is everyone? The golden streets are deserted!"

"Didn't you hear, little one? The Christ Child was born in Bethlehem, and almost everyone has gone to welcome Him."

"The Christ Child! How wonderful!" Angie hurried to the Music Cloud as fast as her chubby little cherub feet would carry her. Even from a distance, she could see the cloud was almost empty. As she grew closer, however, she saw something glistening in the celestial sunlight.

"Oh, no. It can't be!" exclaimed Angie. "They left in such a flurry, they forgot King David's harp! I must take it to them. The performance for the Christ Child

was to be the most magnificent performance of all! It just wouldn't be the same without the most magnificent harp of all."

Angie managed to remove the harp from the case and, holding it tightly under one arm, she ran to the pearly gates. "St. Peter!" Angie called. "They've forgotten King David's harp and I must take it to them!"

"That's a very long trip for such a very small angel," St. Peter said. "I'm afraid I can't give you permission to go. However, I will tell the Almighty God you wish to speak with Him. Wait here, child."

Angie's knees were shaking so badly her robe danced about her knees. Never had she presented herself before God Himself. Soon St. Peter returned.

"All right, child, you may go up. God will see you now."

A warm, golden glow seemed to light up the heavens as Angie approached the Heavenly Throne. Suddenly...there she was...face to face with the Almighty God!

"Hello, Sir. I…I'm very happy about the birth of the Christ Child. You must be very excited and…and very busy! Thank you for seeing me."

"I am pleased. This is the most important day the world has known. But tell me. What brings such a small angel before me this day?"

"Oh, Sir, it's a matter of greatest importance! They've all gone to perform for the Christ Child's birthday, but they've forgotten the most important instrument of all!"

"Mmm. Regrettable, yes…and what shall we do?"

"Well, Sir, if you wouldn't mind, Sir, I would like to take the harp to Earth myself. If I leave now, I could still make it in time! I don't mind the trip, and I would so love to see the Christ Child."

"Yes…I imagine He would like to catch a glimpse of you, too. Very well, you may go. But wait until I write a message for you to give to the Celestial Choirmaster."

"Oh, thank you, Sir! I'll make it! I just know I will!" Angie took the message and began running as fast as she could. Soon she was flying toward Earth with the harp hung over one arm. It was a long trip, and Angie was very tired. Just when she began to think she must have taken a wrong turn somewhere, she saw a glorious light filling the night sky below her. There was the Celestial Choir, preparing to sing to a group of shepherds in the field. They were certainly surprised to see Angie! Before the Choirmaster could scold her for coming, Angie handed him the message from Almighty God! He opened the message and read:

I am very proud of this small angel. Though she knew the journey would be difficult, she was still eager to bring the harp to Earth so my Son might be praised. I am pleased. You are to make a special place for Angie in the Celestial Choir. Be sure it is she who plays King David's harp.

Angie couldn't believe her ears! Quickly, the Choirmaster showed her where to stand. She knew in her heart she could play the harp. After all, if the Almighty God believed she could, she could.

Suddenly a bright light filled the sky. The shepherds looked so afraid, but one of the angels told them to fear not, and gave them the news of the birth of the Christ Child in the City of David. As the choir sang "glory to God in the highest, and on Earth peace, good-will toward men," Angie knew this was her proudest moment. Not only was she playing King David's harp with the Celestial Choir, but the harps had never sounded so perfectly tuned!

"Please, sir, may we fly over Bethlehem on our way back to heaven?" Angie asked the Choirmaster. "I just have to see the Christ Child."

"Certainly, little one. Why else have we come?"

Angie couldn't be perfectly sure, but it seemed to her that as she looked down on the Christ Child there in the manger, He looked right at her and smiled. She felt a warm glow from the top of her head to the tip of her toes. On the trip back to heaven, Angie noticed the harp didn't seem nearly so heavy. Her heart was so full of love for the Christ Child, nothing else mattered.

"If Only It Would Snow"

BY ANDREA DORAY
ILLUSTRATED BY MARK DIXON

I'm waiting on the doorstep
for the snow on Christmas Eve,
but the day is warm and sunny
and I still can't quite believe
that instead of hats and mittens
I am out in my shirt sleeves!

It hardly seems like Christmas
without snowflakes in the air,
twirling, dancing their way down
and landing everywhere,
on trees and lawns and streets and ponds
which now are standing bare!

If just a little bit of snow
were covering the ground,
I might leave funny footprints
in my yard and all around
that anyone could follow—
if I wanted to be found!

At night, the trees would seem to glow
if each and every light
were peeking 'round a bed of snow
to shine so starry-bright,
and Christmas reds and greens and golds
were laced with winter white!

I'd build a fort of icy walls,
(with snowballs just for show!);
make angels lying on my back,
my arms spread to and fro;
catch frosty flakes upon my tongue—
if only it would snow!

I'd like to build some snowmen
and go sledding down the hill,
and watch my breath hang in the air,
so crisp with winter-chill.
At Christmas, it's supposed to snow…
Oh! Do you think it will?

Gifts for the First Birthday

A LEGEND BY RUTH SAWYER • ILLUSTRATED BY CLAUDIA HEASTON

It was winter—and twelve months since the gypsies had driven their flocks of mountain sheep over the dark, gloomy Balkans and settled in the southlands near to the Aegean. It was twelve months since they had seen a wonderful star appear in the sky and heard the singing of angelic voices.

They had marveled much concerning the star until a runner had passed them from the south bringing them news that the star had marked the birth of a Child whom the wise men had hailed as "King of Israel" and "Prince of Peace." This had made Herod of Judea so afraid and angry that he sent soldiers to kill the Child; but in the night the Child and Mary and Joseph had miraculously disappeared—and no one knew whither they had gone. Therefore, Herod had sent runners all over the lands with a message forbidding everyone to give food, shelter, or warmth to the Child, under penalty of death.

Now on that day that marked the end of the twelve months since the star had shone, the gypsies said among themselves, "Dost thou think that the star will shine again tonight? If it shone twelve months ago to mark the place where the Child lay, might it even mark His hiding-place this night? Then Herod would know where to find Him, and send his soldiers again to slay Him. What a cruel thing to happen!"

The air was chill with the winter frost and the gypsies built high their fire and hung their kettle full of millet, fish, and bitter herbs for their supper. The king lay on his couch of tiger-skins, and on his arms were amulets of heavy gold, while rings of gold were on his fingers and in his ears. His tunic was of heavy silk covered with a leopard cloak, and on his feet were shoes of goatskin trimmed with fur. Now, as they feasted around the fire, a voice came to them through the darkness, calling. It was a man's voice, climbing the mountain from the south.

"Ohe! Ohe!" he shouted. And then nearer, "O–he!"

The gypsies were still disputing among themselves whence the voice came when there walked into the circle about the fire a tall, shaggy man, grizzled with age, and a sweet-faced young mother carrying a child.

"We are outcasts," said the man, hoarsely. "Ye must know that whoever succours us will bring Herod's vengeance like a sword about his head. For a year we have wandered homeless and cursed over the world. Only the wild creatures have not feared to share their food and give us shelter in their lairs. But tonight we can go no farther; and we beg the warmth of your fire and food enough to stay us until the morrow."

The king looked at them long before he made reply. He saw the weariness in their eyes and the famine in their cheeks; he saw, as well, the holy light that hung about the Child, and he said at last to his men, "It is the Child of Bethlehem, the one they call the 'Prince of Peace.' As yon man says, who shelters them shelters the wrath of Herod as well. Shall we let them tarry?"

One of their number sprung to his feet, crying, "It is a sin to turn strangers from the fire, a greater sin if they be poor and friendless. And what is a king's wrath to us? I say bid them welcome. What say the rest?"

And with one accord the gypsies shouted, "Yea, let them tarry!"

They brought fresh skins and threw them down beside the fire for the man and woman to rest on. They brought them food and wine and goat's milk for the Child. When they had seen that all was made comfortable for them, they gathered round the Child— these brown gypsy people—to touch His small white hands and feel His golden hair. They brought Him a

chain of gold to play with and another for His neck and tiny arm.

"See, these shall be Thy gifts, little one," said they, "the gifts for Thy first birthday."

And long after all had fallen asleep, the Child sat on His bed of skins beside the blazing fire and watched the light dance on the beads of gold. He laughed and clapped His hands together to see the pretty sight they made.

Soon the Child was fast asleep, and while He slept, a small brown bird hopped out of the thicket. Cocking his little head, he said, "What can I be giving the Child of Bethlehem? I could fetch Him a fat worm to eat or catch Him the beetle that crawls on yonder bush, but He would not like that! And I could tell Him a story of the lands of the north, but He is asleep and would not hear." And the brown bird shook his head quite sorrowfully. Then he saw that the wind was bringing the sparks from the fire nearer and nearer to the sleeping Child.

So the small brown bird spread wide his wings and caught the sparks on his own brown breast. So many sparks fell on him that the feathers were burned; and burned was the flesh beneath until the breast was no longer brown, but red.

The next morning, when the gypsies awoke, they found Mary and Joseph and the Child gone. For Herod had died, and an angel had come in the night and carried them back to the land of Judea.

But the good God blessed those who had cared that night for the Child. And He blessed the brown bird, "Faithful little watcher, from this night forth you and your children shall have red breasts that the world may never forget your gift to the Child of Bethlehem."

Children's French Prayer

ANONYMOUS • ILLUSTRATED BY LINDA CURELL

Little Jesus of the crib,
  Give us the virtues of those who surround you,
  Make us as philosophical as the fisherman,
Carefree as the drummer,
Kind as the ass,
Strong as the ox which keeps you warm.
Give us the sacred leisure of the hunter,
Give us also the desire of the shepherd
  for earthly things,
The pride of the knife grinder and the weaver,
The song of the miller.

Grant us the knowledge of the Magi,
The cheerfulness of the pigeon,
The impulsiveness of the cock,
The discretion of the snail,
The meekness of the lamb.
Give us the goodness of bread,
The tenderness of the wild boar,
The salt of the haddock,
The good humor of old wine,
The radiance of the candle,
The purity of the star.

The Year There Could Be No Christmas

BY ANDREA DORAY • ILLUSTRATED BY KRISTIN KENNEDY SMITH

Dear Diary:

Today was a most very special Christmas Day and I have to tell you all about it because, after all, we thought this was the year there could be no Christmas. Everyone knows Christmas can't happen without my mom. It's my mom who organizes the community bake sale and makes sure there are just the right number of cupcakes and brownies and sugar cookies shaped like stars trees angels bells and all of them covered with thick icing shiny on top. It's my mom who directs the Christmas play at our church and judges the house decorating contest in all the neighborhoods and leads the carolers at the old folks home on one of those really clear and crisp and cold star-twinkly December nights. (For a long time I even believed it was my mom who arranged for the first snowfall on the evening of the Christmas parade so when we all walked to our places along the curb, the snow would crunch under our boots and the lights from the floats—red and green and blue and gold and even brightest white like the very end of a candle flame—would be reflected in the millions and billions of tiny crystals around us.)

But what Mom really does best is Christmas at home. Before Thanksgiving is hardly over, she's already hauling the boxes up from the basement and calling to all of us to help her unpack the goodies: thin glass ornaments—one for each of us kids with our names hand-painted on—and wooden rocking horses and trains with little cars hooked all together and toy soldiers made from clothespins and my very favorite one which is a tiny manger scene that hangs from a gold cord and is complete with little stick figure cows and sheep and Mary and Joseph made of straw and the Baby under a real thatched roof and all of this no bigger than one of those fat green erasers you love to take to school and usually find at the very bottom of

your stocking on Christmas morning just when you think it is finally empty.

And then there's our big dinner on Christmas Day after all of us have opened our packages and gotten at least one of everything we asked for and even a few things we didn't and I have always wondered how our table was going to hold it all because my mom just can't seem to stop herself when she's in the kitchen cooking Christmas dinner.

We have four kinds of salad and two kinds of bread and even three kinds of potatoes—baked and mashed and sweet potatoes with the little marshmallows on top just starting to melt—and always a turkey so big my mom has to have my dad grab the other end of the pan just to lift it out of the oven.

But it's the desserts we all wait for. Dessert at Christmas dinner means something for everyone because there are pumpkin pies with real honest-to-goodness whipped cream for me and Dad and cheesecake with little patterns of reindeer on the top for Lynne and an old-fashioned apple pie because Mom saved some homemade ice cream from our last summer picnic just to serve with it on Christmas Day.

And then after dinner (but somehow before the day is over) my mom has gone through the whole house and gathered up all the stray wrappings and bows and candy canes and pine needles and batteries and shoe laces and fat green erasers that have all found their way to her floor and she still has time to tell us the story of Bethlehem and the stable and the Baby before we go to bed to dream of toy soldiers and stockings and apple pies.

So everyone knows that Christmas just can't happen without my mom. That is, until my mom didn't come home this year.

Nobody knew it at first but this was one Christmas

that wouldn't be like all the others. First it was the bake sale problem. There were too many brownies and not enough cookies and even though everything got sold it just wasn't the same without all those stars and trees and angels and bells. Mom did find time to judge the neighborhood house decorating contest (and the winner was a really great scene of the Three Wise Men with camels and trees and sand dunes cut out of wood and with a light behind them so all you saw were their black outlines like shadows in front of the Star) and to lead us all through "O Come All Ye Faithful" and "We Wish You a Merry Christmas" at the old folks home but when she told Reverend Whitney at the church that she couldn't direct the play this year, Christmas came screeching to a halt.

And all because of a little baby. My mother's sister was having a baby. She couldn't do it at Thanksgiving when we had dinner at Grandma's and my mom only had to help out with the dishes and she couldn't do it on Valentine's Day when you're supposed to have fat little babies even with wings on them and holding big red hearts and arrows—no, she had to do it at Christmas. And of course no one knew exactly when she was going to do it so my mom was always out at her house all the time before Christmas and that's why she couldn't direct the play and that's why there were too many brownies at the sale.

And even though our very own tree wasn't decorated and our stockings were all in a pile beside the fireplace, none of us ever expected Mom to miss Christmas dinner especially because before she left the last time to go to my aunt's house, she brought home the biggest turkey I ever saw and my dad had to help her just to get it in the house.

So when the phone rang last night on Christmas Eve, we all watched Dad as he answered it and we could tell by the look on his face that Mom wasn't on her way home. "All right…all right" he was saying and nodding his head and then "we'll do just fine" and "call us when you have some good news." Then he hung up the phone and turned to us and said "your aunt will probably have the baby tonight so Mom won't be home till she does" and we all hoped it would be soon so the turkey and potatoes and apple pies and cheesecakes would appear like always on Christmas Day.

But then, Dear Diary, it started to snow. It snowed and snowed and snowed and they cancelled the

Christmas parade because it wouldn't stop snowing and it snowed so hard it covered the Star lighting the way for the wooden Three Wise Men and was so deep the camels were covered up past their knees. There was no parade this year and no Star and nothing was even moving so by the time we went to bed on Christmas Eve there were no cars and no trains and no airplanes…and no Mom.

And when we woke up this morning it wasn't the same even though Dad was there and he showed us the packages under the tree which still didn't look like ours and he let us feel our stockings and through the rough thick red wool we knew there were packs of cards and little flashlights and some pencils and fat erasers but all the same we didn't spill everything out on the scratchy bricks by the fireplace because "wait for Mom" we said.

We didn't open any packages and there were no ribbons or wrapping on the floor and when Mrs. Feldon next door stopped by with some slices of ham sweet sticky on top and a round glass dish with cabbage hot and creamy we just pushed our plates away on the big table in the dining room with the tallback chairs and lace hankies on everything.

And the thing is it was that baby's fault my mom didn't come home and there was no Christmas. But when we went up to bed on our pillows tonight there were tiny books and the story was all about a little Baby and the angel said good news good news for everyone because a little Baby was born in the cold and far from home and without parades and trees and turkeys and ice cream saved from the last summer picnic on Labor Day.

So when the phone rang just now we knew it was my mom and she told us "it's a boy and he's fine and it's snowing and love love love to everyone, I'll come home when I can so Merry Christmas—he's beautiful—I miss you…Merry Christmas Merry Christmas."

And so now, Dearest Diary, when we talk about our special Christmases, we will still say remember the year we had three pumpkin pies and remember the year not a creature was stirring except for the mouse that ran straight up the trunk of the tree on Christmas Eve and remember when it never snowed at all and we played stickball on the yellow prickly lawn after dinner. But I will always say remember the year it snowed so hard and it covered the Star and Mom didn't come home but it was good news good news for everyone because a little Baby was born.

A Letter From Santa Claus

BY MARK TWAIN • ILLUSTRATED BY R. DEAN GRIST

Palace of St. Nicholas
In the Moon
Christmas Morning

My Dear Susie Clemens:

I have received and read all the letters which you and your little sister have written me with the help of your mother. I have also read those which you little people have written me with your own hands. Although you did not use any characters that are in grown peoples' alphabet, you used the characters that all children in all lands on earth and in the twinkling stars use. And, since all my subjects in the moon are children, you will easily understand that I can read you and your baby sister's jagged and fantastic marks without any trouble at all. But I had trouble with those letters you dictated through your mother.

You will find that I made no mistakes about the things which you and the baby ordered in your own letters. I went down your chimney at midnight, when you were asleep, and delivered them all myself—kissed both of you, too, because you are good children, well-trained, nice-mannered, and about the most obedient little people I ever saw. But in the letter which you dictated, there were some words I could not make out, and one or two small orders I could not fill because we ran out of stock. Our last lot of kitchen furniture for dolls has just gone to a very poor little child in the North Star way up in the cold country above the Big Dipper.

Dear Santa Claus, I am writing for Susie Clemens who asked me to tell you what a good girl she's been this past year.

There was a word or two in your mama's letter which I couldn't be certain of. I took it to be a "trunk full of doll's clothes." Is that it? I will call at your kitchen door about nine o'clock this morning to inquire. But I must not see anybody and I must not speak to anybody but you. You must go up to the nursery and stand on a chair and put your ear to the speaking tube that leads down to the kitchen, and when I whistle through it, you must speak in the tube and say, "Welcome, Santa Claus!" Then I will ask whether it was a trunk you ordered or not. If you say it was, I shall ask you what color you want the trunk to be. Your mama will help you to name a nice color and then you must tell me every single thing in detail which you want the trunk to contain. Then when I say, "Goodbye and a Merry Christmas to my little Susie Clemens," you must say, "Goodbye, good old Santa Claus, I thank you very much."

Tell everyone to keep quiet till I go back up the chimney. You may then go and peep through the dining room doors, and you will see the thing which you want, right under the piano in the drawing room—for I shall have put it there.

Goodbye, for a few minutes, till I come down to the world and ring the kitchen doorbell.

Your loving,

Santa Claus

Christmas Leftovers

BY CONNIE KALE JOHNSON • ILLUSTRATED BY PAM FOUTS

Click! The toy shop became dark! Creak! The door closed and the room filled with silence.

"The toy maker can't go home yet!" shouted Sergeant, the royal palace guard.

"But he has!" cried Sandy Bear, sitting next to him on the workbench. "And he forgot to finish getting us ready for Christmas."

"Who wants a royal guard without his jacket under their tree?" sputtered Sergeant marching back and forth.

"Or a teddy bear without all her stuffing?" sobbed the skinny bear struggling to sit up straight.

The sniffles and tears and stomping of wooden boots filled the shop while snowflakes touched the shop window that once held toys.

"I wish we were going to someone's house for Christmas," sighed Sandy, watching the snow dance around the village lamp post.

Without warning, the flakes began to swirl and whirl in a spinning wind. And then— Creak! Bang! The door blew open.

"Up on your feet, Sandy!" ordered the guard, pulling on Sandy's paw. "We're getting out of here!"

"Where are we going?" asked the worried, sad-looking bear.

"Shopping for a home," answered the Sergeant, marching arm and arm out of the shop with his friend, Sandy Bear.

The snow was getting deeper and deeper as they walked through the tree-surrounded village. The harsh wind whipped around their heads as they trudged onward, past the darkened shop windows.

After many minutes, Sandy snapped, "I'm not taking another step!" and she plopped her furry tail on the street curb.

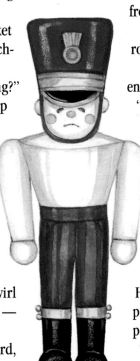

"Wanna bet?" shouted Sergeant. "Look what's coming!"

"Woof, Woof!" barked a huge, fierce dog crossing the street.

Grabbing Sandy's paw, Sergeant raced toward an alley. Sandy felt her body swing around the corner with her feet in mid-air, the snarling dog just inches from her paws.

"Clang! Rattle! Bang!" A garbage can went rolling end over end.

"Meow! Yeow!" Out jumped a very frightened cat.

"Woof! Woof!" And a new chase down Main Street began.

Escaping over the top of a snow drift, Sandy and Sergeant stopped to rest. "I'm sorry you don't have a coat," Sandy sighed, putting her arms around the shivering guard. "You're so brave."

"I'm only doing my duty," sputtered Sergeant, shyly.

The chimes in the clock on top of City Hall began ringing carols through the tall pines. The snow stopped and a bright star peeked around a passing cloud.

"Listen, it's almost Christmas!" cried the weary bear. "Here we are, nothing but homeless Christmas leftovers."

"Now, Sandy, don't be too sure about that...look at those flickering lights between those trees over there."

"What lights? I don't see anything. Are you sure it's not just moonbeams playing tricks on us?"

"We can't find out from here. Come on!" ordered the guard pulling the bear to her feet.

Shivering in snow up to their knees, the weary friends reached a cottage deep in the woods. They peeked through a cracked board in the door.

"Oh," sighed Sandy, "the little boy and girl in front of the fireplace look so sad..."

"That must be their mother and father sitting at the bare table," whispered Sergeant. "I don't see a sign of Christmas anywhere."

"Not even a tree," said Sandy.

"Or a toy," quietly answered the guard. "S-h-h! I think they heard us!"

The bear and the sergeant huddled together as the sound of footsteps approached the door. The brass knob turned, the door swung open, and the flickering firelight shone down on the lonely toys.

"Papa," whispered the mother, "gifts for the children!" With a twinkle in their eyes, the parents turned to the little boy and girl.

"Now, off to bed with you, children. Tomorrow is Christmas, you know!"

"But, Mama...?"

"Listen to your mother. Goodnight, children," said the papa.

The children meekly went off to bed.

After the children were sound asleep, Papa went outside and returned with a small tree. He took his large, colorful neckerchief and tore it into narrow strips which he tied in bows on the tree's branches. Mama hummed while she sewed a brand-new jacket for Sergeant. By the time she finished stuffing Sandy, it was late into the night.

"Wake up, you sleepyheads!" Papa called in his husky voice. "Are you going to sleep Christmas away?"

"It's Christmas! It's Christmas!" shouted the children, hugging their gifts.

For the first time, Sandy felt like a lovable roly-poly teddy bear and Sergeant stood at proud attention in his royal palace uniform. And they knew in their hearts that they would never feel like Christmas leftovers again.

The Twelve Days of Christmas

A TRADITIONAL CAROL • ILLUSTRATED BY TIM O'TOOLE

The **first** day of Christmas
My true love sent to me
A partridge in a pear tree.

The **second** day of Christmas
My true love sent to me
Two turtle doves
And a partridge in a pear tree.

The **third** day of Christmas
My true love sent to me
Three French hens,
Two turtle doves,
And a partridge in a pear tree.

The **fourth** day of Christmas
My true love sent to me
Four colly birds,
Three French hens,
Two turtle doves,
And a partridge in a pear tree.

The **fifth** day of Christmas
My true love sent to me
Five gold rings,
Four colly birds,
Three French hens,
Two turtle doves,
And a partridge in a pear tree.

The **sixth** day of Christmas
My true love sent to me
Six geese a-laying,
Five gold rings,
Four colly birds,
Three French hens,
Two turtle doves,
And a partridge in a pear tree.

The **seventh** day of Christmas
My true love sent to me
Seven swans a-swimming,
Six geese a-laying,
Five gold rings,
Four colly birds,
Three French hens,
Two turtle doves,
And a partridge in a pear tree.

The **eighth** day of Christmas
My true love sent to me
Eight maids a-milking,
Seven swans a-swimming,
Six geese a-laying,
Five gold rings,
Four colly birds,
Three French hens,
Two turtle doves,
And a partridge in a pear tree.

The **eleventh** day of Christmas
My true love sent to me
Eleven ladies dancing,
Ten pipers piping,
Nine drummers drumming,
Eight maids a-milking,
Seven swans a-swimming
Six geese a-laying,
Five gold rings,
Four colly birds,
Three French hens,
Two turtledoves,
And a partridge in a pear tree.

The **ninth** day of Christmas
My true love sent to me
Nine drummers drumming,
Eight maids a-milking,
Seven swans a-swimming,
Six geese a-laying,
Five gold rings,
Four colly birds,
Three French hens,
Two turtle doves,
And a partridge in a pear tree.

The **twelfth** day of Christmas
My true love sent to me
Twelve lords a-leaping,
Eleven ladies dancing,
Ten pipers piping,
Nine drummers drumming,
Eight maids a-milking,
Seven swans a-swimming,
Six geese a-laying,
Five gold rings,
Four colly birds,
Three French hens,
Two turtle doves,
And a partridge in a pear tree.

The **tenth** day of Christmas
My true love sent to me
Ten pipers piping,
Nine drummers drumming,
Eight maids a-milking,
Seven swans a-swimming,
Six geese a-laying,
Five gold rings,
Four colly birds,
Three French hens,
Two turtledoves,
And a partridge in a pear tree.

dog, and that's just how Mr. Dog felt. By and by, he went sound asleep right there in his chair, with all his Santa Claus clothes on.

There he sat, all night long, and even when it came morning he slept right on. Then pretty soon Mr. 'Possum poked his head out. Then Mr. Crow and Mr. Raccoon did, too. They all looked toward the stockings, and they didn't see Mr. Dog, or even each other. They saw their stockings though, and Mr. Raccoon said all at once, "Oh, there's something in my stocking!"

And Mr. Crow said, "Oh, there's something in my stocking, too!"

And Mr. 'Possum said, "Oh, there's something in all our stockings!"

And with that, they all gave a great hurrah together, and rushed out and grabbed their stockings and turned around just in time to see Mr. Dog jump straight up out of his chair, for he did not know the least bit where in the world he was.

"Oh, there's Santa Claus himself!" they all shouted together and made a rush for their rooms, for they were scared almost to death. But it all dawned on Mr. Dog in a second, and he began to laugh to think what a joke it was on everybody. And when they heard Mr. Dog laugh, they knew it was him right away; and they all came out, and he had to tell just what he'd done. So they emptied their stockings and ate some of the presents and looked at others until they almost forgot about breakfast, just as children do on Christmas morning.

Then Mr. Crow said he'd make a little hot cocoa, and that Mr. Dog must stay and have some, and by and by they made him promise to spend the day with them. It was snowing hard outside, and it snowed so hard that Mr. Dog decided to stay all night, and after dinner they all sat around the fire and told stories. And Mr. Crow and Mr. 'Possum and Mr. Raccoon had the very nicest Christmas that ever was in the Hollow Tree or in the Big Deep Woods anywhere.

The Little Match Girl

BY HANS CHRISTIAN ANDERSEN
ILLUSTRATED BY PAM PELTIER

It was late on a bitterly cold, snowy, New Year's Eve. A poor little girl was wandering in the dark cold streets; she was bareheaded and barefooted. She certainly had had shoes on when she left home, but they were not much good, for they were so huge. They had last been worn by her mother, and they fell off the poor little girl's feet when she was running across the street to avoid two carriages that were rolling rapidly by. One of the shoes could not be found at all; and the other was picked up by a boy who ran off with it, saying that it would do for a cradle when he had children of his own. So the poor little girl had to go on with her little bare feet, which were blue with the cold. She carried a quantity of matches in her apron, and held a packet of them in her hand. Nobody had bought any from her during all the long day; nobody had even given her a copper.

The poor little creature was hungry and perishing with cold, and she looked the picture of misery. The snowflakes fell upon her long yellow hair, which curled so prettily round her face, but she paid no attention to that. Lights were shining from every window, and there was a most delicious odour of roast goose in the streets, for it was New Year's Eve—she could not forget that. She found a protected place where one house projected a little beyond the next one, and here she crouched, drawing up her feet under her, but she was colder than ever. She did not dare to go home, for she had not sold any matches and had not earned a single penny. Besides, it was

almost as cold at home as it was here. They lived in a house where the wind whistled through every crack, although they tried to stuff up the biggest ones with rags and straw. Her tiny hands were almost paralyzed with cold. Oh, if she could only find some way to warm them!

Dare she pull one match out of the bundle and strike it on the wall to warm her fingers? She pulled one out. "Ritsch!" How it sputtered, how it blazed! It burnt with a bright clear flame, just like a little candle when she held her hand round it. It was a very curious candle, too. The little girl fancied that she was sitting in front of a big stove with polished brass feet and handles. There was a splendid fire blazing in it and warming her so beautifully, but—what happened? Just as she was stretching out her feet to warm them, the blaze went out, the stove vanished, and she was left sitting with the end of the burnt-out match in her hand. She struck a new one, it burnt, it blazed up, and where the light fell upon the wall against which she lay, it became transparent like gauze, and she could see right through it into the room inside. There was a table spread with a snowy cloth and pretty china; a roast goose stuffed with apples and prunes was steaming on it. And what was even better, the goose hopped from the dish and waddled across the

floor! It came right up to the poor child, and then—the match went out and there was nothing to be seen but the thick black wall.

She lit another match. This time she was sitting under a lovely Christmas tree. It was much bigger and more beautifully decorated than the one she had seen when she had peeped through the glass doors at the rich merchant's house this Christmas day. Thousands of lighted candles gleamed upon its branches, and coloured pictures such as she had seen in the shop windows looked down upon her. The little girl stretched out her hands toward them, then out went the match. All the Christmas candles rose higher and higher, till she saw that they were only the twinkling stars. One of them fell and made a bright streak of light across the sky. "Someone is dying," thought the little girl; for her grandmother used to say, "When a star falls, a soul is going up to God."

Now she struck another match against the wall, and this time it was her grandmother who appeared in the circle of flame. She saw her quite clearly and distinctly, looking so gentle and happy.

"Grandmother!" cried the little girl. "Oh, do take me with you! I know you will vanish when the match goes out; you will vanish like the warm stove, the delicious goose, and the beautiful Christmas tree!"

She hastily struck a whole bundle of matches, because she did so want to keep her grandmother with her. The light of the matches made it as bright as day. Grandmother had never before looked so big or so beautiful. She lifted the little girl up in her arms, and they soared in a halo of light and joy, far, far above the earth, where there was no more cold, no hunger, no pain, for they were with God.

The Skinny Scrawny Christmas Tree

BY SUSAN SWANSON SWARTZ • ILLUSTRATED BY K. GUS ALAVEZOS

"Tonight we're bringing home our Christmas tree!" Jonathan told Marie as they walked home from school. "It's really huge…just wait till you see it!"

Marie smiled. Jonathan's family always had a huge tree full of branches, the kind of tree so thick you couldn't even see through it! Marie wished her parents would get one like that. Every year their tree was the same—one of those skinny, scrawny, spindly looking things—that her mom said was a tradition.

Marie waved goodbye to Jonathan at the gate to her house. As she walked up the sidewalk, she gazed at the living room window. Just once she would like to see a big, fat, full tree in her window!

Inside, Marie found a note from her mom: "Dear Marie, I will be back by 4:00…you can snack on milk and cookies! Love, Mom." Marie shed her winter clothes and took her snack into the living room. She flopped on the couch and daydreamed about a full, "perfect" Christmas tree. Everyone in the neighborhood would see the magnificent tree through the window! Marie imagined her tree was the most beautiful tree in the whole world.

Marie's daydreams were interrupted when her mom came home. "Hi! I see you found the milk and cookies," her mom said. "You'll need some energy because, in half an hour, we're meeting your dad to pick out our tree!"

Marie didn't answer. "Oh, boy," she thought, "another skinny, scrawny Christmas tree!"

"You know," her mom said, "maybe this year we should get a different kind of tree…one of those big, full trees you've always wanted. What do you think?"

Marie couldn't believe her ears! A change in tradition? A fat, full, gorgeously perfect tree?

"Do you really mean it?" she asked. "We can have one of those big, full trees?"

"If that's what you really want," her mom replied, smiling at Marie's excitement.

All the way on the drive to meet her dad, Marie kept imagining the beautiful tree she would choose. When they arrived, she raced to the fenced-in area to see all the trees. "Lead the way, Marie!" her dad said.

Marie wandered through the maze of trees, all standing so majestically with their perfect triangle Christmas-tree shapes. First, she chose one with long needles. Then she liked the short-needled one better. One was taller and fatter, but the other one looked more like a Christmas tree.

"I can't decide!" Marie exclaimed.

"That's fine, take your time," her dad said with a chuckle.

"We'll just wait here while you make up your mind," her mom said.

"Great! Thanks!" Marie said. Then she spotted the perfect tree. It was at least seven feet tall and almost that big around! As she stood admiring it, another taller one caught her eye. "This tree is definitely the tallest one I have found so far," she thought. "It's beautiful!"

"I think you will be our tree!" Marie said.

As she walked around and around the tall beautiful tree, she noticed some more trees just flopped against the fence. "Those must be the rejects," Marie thought. She felt sorry for the trees on the fence. They looked so lonely and sad. They certainly didn't look like all the other magnificent Christmas trees!

Marie walked over to the sad-looking trees. She pulled a short one with two top branches from the group. "You poor tree! No one would ever want a short tree with two tops!" Marie thought. She looked over at the tall, full one she had chosen, then back to the one in her mittened hand.

"You certainly aren't a tall, full tree, and you have a rather funny top, but you are really kind of beautiful," she said. "But I came here to get a *perfect* tree. You're too scrawny…I want a big, full one this year."

Marie looked back and forth at both trees. Then she took a deep breath, sighed, and said, "I know which tree I really want! You are scrawny and skinny, but after I put ornaments and lights on you, you will be the most beautiful tree in the world!"

Marie went back to get her mom and dad. As she led them to her tree, they passed the tree with the long needles, and the tree with the short needles, the big, fat tree, and the tall, full tree.

"What is this?" her dad asked, his face full of surprise when they stopped at Marie's tree.

"Where is your big, full tree?" her mom asked. Marie held up the skinny, scrawny Christmas tree and said happily, "This is our perfect tree!"

Once in Royal David's City

BY CECIL FRANCIS ALEXANDER
ILLUSTRATED BY DONALD TWO OTTER

Once in royal David's city
   Stood a lowly cattle shed,
   Where a mother laid her Baby
  In a manger for His bed:
Mary was that mother mild,
Jesus Christ, her little Child.

He came down to earth from Heaven,
   Who is God and Lord of all,
And His shelter was a stable,
   And His cradle was a stall:
With the poor and mean and lowly,
Lived on earth our Savior Holy.

And, through all His wondrous childhood,
   He would honor and obey,
Love and watch the lowly maiden
   In whose gentle arms He lay;
Christian children all must be
Mild, obedient, good as He.

For He is our childhood's pattern;
   Day by day like us He grew;
He was little, weak, and helpless,
   Tears and smiles like us He knew;
And he feeleth for our sadness,
And He shareth in our gladness.

And our eyes at last shall see Him,
   Through His own redeeming love;
For that Child so dear and gentle
   Is our Lord in Heaven above;
And He leads His children on
To the place where He is gone.

Not in that poor lowly stable,
    With the oxen standing by,
We shall see Him; but in Heaven,
    Set at God's right hand on high;
When, like stars, His children crowned,
All in white, shall wait around.

The Legend of the Poinsettia

ANONYMOUS
ILLUSTRATED BY CARY HEATH

It seems that one Christmas Eve, long, long ago, a young Mexican boy who was very poor approached the village church. He had no gift to bring to the Christ Child and he was terribly sad. Because he had no gift, the little boy was afraid to enter the church, and he fell down on his knees outside the door instead. He prayed to God, assuring Him with heartfelt tears of his love for the Christ Child.

"I am very poor and am afraid to approach the Babe with empty hands," he explained in his prayers.

Just then, the little boy saw at his feet a green plant with gorgeous petals of dazzling red. He broke some of the beautiful flowers from the plant and proudly entered the church to lay his remarkable gift at the feet of the Christ Child.

Since then, the story goes, the plant spread over the land. In America, we call it the Christmas flower, and enjoy its beauty each year as we celebrate the Saviour's birth.

Little Grey Rabbit's Christmas

BY ALISON UTTLEY • ILLUSTRATED BY SHARON SANDNER CARTWRIGHT

"I think I shall take out the sledge and toboggan down the hill by moonlight," said Hare, looking up at the round moon which made the land bright as day. "I might see something of Santa Claus and his reindeer."

He wrapped a muffler round his neck, seized the cord of the brand new scarlet-coloured sledge Grey Rabbit had just given to him and Squirrel and ran across the fields to the hill. Then down he swooped, flying like a bird.

Everything looked different in the white moon-beams. The ice crackled, the stars sparkled and winked at the excited Hare. Again and again he rushed down the hill, his eyes on the lovely moon. Suddenly he noticed a shadow running alongside it. It was his own moon-shadow, but Hare saw the long ears and round head of a strange monster.

"Oh dear! Who is that dusky fellow racing by my side?" he cried.

He took to his heels, leaving the sledge lying in the field, and away he went, running from his own shadow. He listened a moment, but there was only the "too-whit, too-whoo" of Wise Owl somewhere deep in the wood, and the frightened Hare hurried home.

"Did you come without the sledge?" demanded Squirrel indignantly. "Hare! You are a coward! You ran away from your own shadow! You've lost our lovely sledge!"

"Better than losing my lovely life," retorted Hare. He felt rather miserable. Shadows were good companions, and he had run away and deserted the scarlet sledge.

"I suppose we had better go to bed," he muttered as he went upstairs gloomily.

The next morning Robin the Postman flew to the door with some Christmas cards and a letter. The little bird rested while Hare examined the leaf with its tiny pointed scribble.

"It's from Mole," said he, twisting it over and over.

"You're reading it upside down, Hare!" cried Squirrel impatiently. She took the little letter and read the scrawl. "Come tonight. Love from Moldy Warp."

"It's a party!" cried Hare. "Quick, Grey Rabbit! Write and say we'll all be there, and we hope there will be plenty to eat. I hope Rat won't be there, though! Ugh!"

The three animals wrapped themselves up in warm clothes, and started for Mole's house. In their baskets they had gifts for their lonely friend, Mole.

"What a pity you lost our beautiful sledge! We could have ridden on it tonight," said Squirrel to Hare.

Hare hung his head. He wished she wouldn't talk about it so much.

When the three got near Mole's house, they saw something glittering. A lighted tree grew by the path, like a burning beacon.

"It's a magical tree, a tree from Fairyland growing in our wood!" whispered Grey Rabbit.

On every branch of the little fir tree, candles wavered their tongues of flame. Little red and gold fruits hung from the boughs. On the ground under the branches were bowls of hazelnuts, loaves of barley bread, piles of wheat cakes, small sacks of corn, platters of berries, and jars of clover honey. Icicles shone like diamonds among the branches, brightly coloured feathers and shells were fastened to the bark, and chains of frozen waterdrops swung to and fro, reflecting the candlelight. On the tip-top of this wonderful tree gleamed the glorious Christmas Star.

"What do you think of my tree?" asked Moldy Warp, stepping out of the shadows.

"Beau-u-u-tiful," they murmured.

"It's not a rose tree, nor a holly tree, nor an apple

tree. Is it a Fairy Tree, Mole?" asked Grey Rabbit.

"It's a Christmas Tree," replied Mole in his soft mysterious voice. "It's for all the birds and beasts of the woods and fields. They will see it from afar and come here. Now sit quietly and watch."

Across the snowy fields padded little dark creatures, all filled with curiosity to see the glowing lights in the tree. The family of Milkman Hedgehog trudged through the snowdrifts. The carollers and market people were there, and Water Rat in his brown velvet coat. Even Wise Owl flew down to see what was the matter, and Rat with his wife and baby stood on the edge of the crowd.

"Help yourselves!" cried Mole. "It is Christmas. Eat and drink and warm yourselves. Take as much as you want for your storerooms."

Then every little creature ate the good food and carried away little bags and baskets of meal and cakes and corn. When they had finished, there was nothing left except the glowing candles which the wind could not extinguish.

From behind a tree, Rat sidled toward Grey Rabbit and touched his hat.

"Miss Grey Rabbit," said he, "I found a scarlet sledge in the field last night, and my Missis read your family name on it, so I took the liberty of bringing it here for you."

"Oh, thank you, kind Rat!' cried Grey Rabbit, delightedly clapping her paws.

"My Missis helped me to drag it along," added Rat. He took Grey Rabbit to the sledge and then he hurried away to his family.

"The sledge is found! Come, Hare! Squirrel! Moldy Warp! Wise Owl! Come and see our sledge," called Grey Rabbit. Everyone crowded round to admire it.

The little scarlet sledge was clean and bright, for Rat had rubbed the snow away. On the top was a fleecy shawl covering something, and Grey Rabbit drew from under it three objects, wonderingly.

The first was a walking stick, made of holly-wood, polished like ivory, and the handle was carved in the shape of Hare.

"That must be for me from Santa Claus," said Hare, seizing the stick.

The second was a little wooden spoon with a hazelnut carved in the handle.

"That is certainly mine," said Squirrel and she put it in her pocket.

The third was a wee box, and when Grey Rabbit unfastened the lid, there was a tiny white thimble inside which fit her little thumb perfectly.

"And I've never had a thimble since Wise Owl swallowed mine," said Grey Rabbit happily.

"Only one person could make such delicate carvings," said Grey Rabbit.

"And that is Rat," said Squirrel.

"They are peace offerings," suggested Mole.

"For Christmas-tide," added Old Hedgehog wisely.

"Three cheers for Rat!" they all cheered. "Hip! Hip! Hurrah!"

Squirrel and Grey Rabbit climbed on the sledge, and Hare drew them over the snow.

"Goodnight. A happy Christmas!" they called. Soon the sledge caught up with a little band of carollers. Their voices rang clear and silvery through the air, and this is what Grey Rabbit heard:

Holly red and mistletoe white,
Peace on earth and mercy bright,
A truce by the tree of candlelight,
Holly red and mistletoe white.

Mistletoe white and holly red,
The day is over, we're off to bed,
Tired body and sleepy head,
Mistletoe white and holly red.

"Peace on earth and mercy bright," Grey Rabbit's heart sang, and Hare ran swiftly over the frozen snow, drawing the scarlet-coloured sledge toward the little house at the end of the wood.

The Year of the Bicycle

BY CHERIE RAYBURN • ILLUSTRATED BY CLAUDIA HEASTON

"Bummer!" I thought when Jimmy blew past me on his new bike. I had to be the only kid in eighth grade without a mountain bike, and my determination to have one grew as Jimmy got smaller in the distance.

The object of my determination was the Trek 820 in the window of Criterium Bike Shop. I walked by it every day, and every day I prayed that the $400 price tag would miraculously change to $40 or $4.

But it never did, and I finally had to face the fact that if that bike were going to be mine, I would have to earn $400.

But how? It was the last week of the school year, and all the great jobs were already taken. I was thinking that it looked like another summer of mowing lawns, when a "Help Wanted" sign caught my eye. I did a double-take—then realized it was in the window of Brookside Retirement Center.

Disappointed, I walked on past the building, but the vision of racing Jimmy on a brand new Trek 820 made me stop and turn around. With a big sigh, I walked back to Brookside, opened the door, and went in.

At the end of the lobby, I found a door with the sign "Office" on it. I knocked and opened it when a voice answered, "Come on in." Sitting behind a big desk was a lady about my mother's age, glasses perched on top of her head, a pencil stuck behind her ear. She smiled and said, "What can I do for you?"

"My name is David Gilbert. I saw your sign, and I really need to earn some money."

"Have a seat, David. I'm Maureen Porter, the manager here, and, yes, we do need some part-time help from now through December 1—doing various odd jobs for us about eight hours a week. The pay is $4 an hour. Interested?"

Doing some quick arithmetic in my head, I realized that by December, I'd have more than enough money for the bike. "I'll take it."

My first day on the job, I had to empty all the residents' trash cans, beginning with apartment #12. Knocking on the door, I read the nameplate—"J. Pulaski." Someone on the other side said, "Ja, ja. Come in."

I opened the door and discovered a white-haired man seated at a desk, reading a newspaper. "Ach, you must be the new boy," he said in a thick, unfamiliar accent.

"I'm just here to empty the trash."

"Is over there, boy—by the dresser."

As I bent down to pick up the trash can, I noticed a silver frame on top of the antique dresser. The old, yellowing photograph it held was the portrait of a family—father and mother sitting; a girl, holding a straw hat, standing by the mother; and a boy, holding a violin, standing by the father. It was amazing how much the boy looked like me—we could have been twins! It was creepy!

"Th-thanks, uh, see you tomorrow," I said nervously as I opened the door to leave.

"Ja, ja," said the old man, absorbed in his paper.

I emptied the other residents' trash cans, then vacuumed the lobby. But I couldn't get that photograph out of my mind. After completing all the day's chores, I stopped by Mrs. Porter's office.

"So, David, how was your first day?" she asked.

"Fine. I think I can handle the work okay. See you tomorrow." I turned to go, then turned back. "Mrs. Porter?"

"Yes, David."

"The man who lives in apartment twelve…"

"You mean Josef Pulaski?"

"Yeah. He sure has a funny accent—what is it?"

"Oh, he's Polish. He's been in America for fifty years, but he still has an accent. He's a very interesting man, David—I think you'd enjoy getting to know him."

"Sure," I said. But I was thinking, "You gotta be kidding! I'm here to earn some money, buy a Trek 820, then beat it. I'm not gonna be wasting any time getting to know anybody, especially some old guy I can hardly even understand!"

But all the way home, and all the next day at school, Josef Pulaski and that picture in the silver frame stuck in my mind.

That afternoon, I again knocked on Mr. Pulaski's door. "Ja, ja. Come in, please." He was sitting at his desk again, but this time he was busy writing. "Oh, is you. I am just writing a letter."

"To your sister?"

"What? What did you say, boy?" He looked startled.

"I-I mean, yesterday I saw this picture on your dresser, and I was thinking that the boy is you, and the girl is your sister…sorry, I don't mean to be rude."

"Oh, I see. That's okay, boy. What's your name, boy?"

"David."

He squinted his eyes and adjusted his glasses to get a better look at me.

"How old are you?"

"Fourteen."

"Hmmm. Most interesting…Is how old I am when that photograph is taken."

"When was it taken?"

"In September, 1943." He took a deep breath. "Just before the Nazis discover we are hiding two Jewish families in our barn. Three months later, Christmas Eve it is, I am playing 'Silent Night' on my violin. Is bitter cold outside, but I stand near an open window, and I play very loud so our Jewish friends can hear the music.

"Suddenly, five Nazi soldiers break in the door. They scream at us…'Jew Lovers' and 'Resistance Pigs,' they say. One soldier holds his gun on us, and the others demolish everything…everything."

Mr. Pulaski paused, took off his glasses to wipe his eyes, then continued.

"I never forget the smile on one soldier's face—he is not much older than I—when he snatch my violin from my hands and smash it—smash it again and again—on the floor…it is a million tiny pieces…"

With great effort, as if the memory made him weak, Mr. Pulaski pulled himself up out of his chair, walked over to the dresser, and gently touched the precious photo of his family.

"That Christmas Eve is last time I see my family. They die in the camps. We were very close, my sister and I. Her name is Christina."

We both stood, silent. I thought I should say something, but words wouldn't come.

Next thing I knew, Mrs. Porter was standing in the door. "David, don't forget to vacuum the front lobby before you leave tonight." Seizing the opportunity, I mumbled, "Bye, Mr. Pulaski, see you tomorrow," and hurried out the door.

That night, I took the giant book about World War II off the shelf in the den. Flipping through its pages, I was stunned by the pictures of Nazi work camps, where millions of people, including Mr. Pulaski's family, suffered and died. And there was one picture—boys my age in thin, pajama-like, striped shirts and pants, barefooted, standing at attention in the snow. Their heads were shaved, cheeks sunken, eyes hollow and dark. I couldn't believe that Mr. Pulaski had actually been in a place like this…I tried to imagine myself in that picture, but it was just too horrifying.

I could hardly wait for the dismissal bell at school. I wanted to get all my jobs done at Brookside so I could visit with Mr. Pulaski before it was time to go home.

It had become routine for me to spend a few minutes every evening with Mr. Pulaski. From Brookside's porch, we watched the days grow shorter and the leaves turn red and gold as we sat and talked. I was

fascinated by his tales of Poland—of growing up on a potato farm, taking violin lessons from an old maestro, hiking with Christina in the hills. Sometimes the memories made his blue eyes sparkle with delight; other times, they glistened with tears.

I didn't realize how quickly the fall had gone by until one day, as I was passing by Mrs. Porter's office, I heard her call, "David, do you have a second?" I went in and sat down. "David, you've been such a tremendous help to us, but it's almost the first of December, and your job will be completed then. I hope you've earned enough money to buy your bicycle."

I had, indeed, earned enough money for the bike, and on the way home, I stopped by the bicycle shop to see it. It was beautiful! The other kids would be so envious—and Mr. Pulaski would be so impressed!

I was daydreaming about racing with Jimmy as I walked home. But when I passed by Ace's Pawn Shop, something in the window caught my eye.

It was a violin. It reminded me of the one in Mr. Pulaski's photograph. Fascinated, I went in and asked to look at it.

"Now how come a kid like you would be interested in that old thing?" the store manager asked. "I bet it's at least fifty years old."

"Where did it come from?"

"How should I know? Probably from one of those countries in Europe—isn't that where all fiddles come from?"

I laughed and put the violin back.

At the first of December, I left my job at Brookside, but I still went to visit Mr. Pulaski every chance I got, and Mrs. Porter invited me to all their holiday events.

I was especially looking forward to the Christmas Eve party. The residents had drawn names for gag gifts, and there would be lots of food.

Mr. Johnson, who made a perfect Santa, handed out the gifts. After everyone had received one, he said, "Wait, someone must not have gotten a gift—there's still a package under the tree, way in the back." As he pulled it out, he read the tag: "'To Josef Pulaski.' Doesn't say who it's from."

"But you give me my gift already," Mr. Pulaski said, puzzled.

"I don't know…it's got your name on it…" Mr. Johnson handed him the large package.

Everyone's attention was suddenly glued to this mystery gift as Mr. Pulaski carefully removed the box's red wrapping and lid. He gasped when he saw its contents. There was silence in the room. Mr. Pulaski sat, just staring into the box, then looked up and met my eyes. "David, David, I cannot believe it…I do not know what to say…"

"What is it?" asked Mrs. Browning, who was about to burst from curiosity. In response, Mr. Pulaski gently lifted an old violin and bow from its case, as if he were lifting a baby from a cradle.

Tears blurred my vision. "Please, Mr. Pulaski, play 'Silent Night' for us—and for Christina."

Without a word, he positioned the instrument under his chin and softly played the old carol. Although it was obvious he hadn't played a violin in a very long time, everyone thought it was the most beautiful song they had ever heard.

As I listened, I thought about my Trek 820—still standing in the bicycle shop window—and I smiled. Maybe next year.

A Pritchard Family Christmas

BY VICKI J. KUYPER • ILLUSTRATED BY JAN GREGG

It looked like the Pritchards had done it again.

"I don't believe it…" I heard my mother tell the neighbors.

"They've really outdone themselves this year," one replied.

"After all this time, I guess we shouldn't expect any less," said another. She shook her head at the jumble of plastic elves and colored lights that filled the Pritchard's front yard. "After Halloween, I really thought they'd learned their lesson."

It was true this Halloween had been a disaster. The Pritchards spent most of October stringing candy corn to hang from their roof and carving pumpkins to line their driveway. But on Halloween night, the Pritchard's cat, while batting a dangling strand of candy corn, accidentally landed in a jack-o'-lantern and singed her tail. Leaping to her escape, she knocked the pumpkin on its side, setting the first sheet of a whole row of hanging ghosts on fire. At least that's how the neighbors tell it. The fire department saved the Pritchard's house, but the driveway of smoky-black jack-o'-lanterns smelled like pumpkin pie for weeks.

"Just getting the neighborhood ready for Thanksgiving!" joked Mr. Pritchard. Mr. Pritchard was always joking.

My mom calls the Pritchard family "eccentric." But you know, I kind of like them. They always seem to have such a good time together. They celebrate everything from Groundhog Day right down to the birthdays of their gerbils.

But every year at Christmastime is when the Pritchards really shine. I mean *really* shine. You've never seen so many lights! Red ones, green ones, white ones, gold ones, twinkly ones, blinking ones, big ones, small ones. They even have lights that go on and off to the music that comes from the big yellow star on the roof while a host of nearby angels keep time by flapping their mechanical wings.

Down on the ground, the Pritchard's front yard looks just like you'd imagine Santa's workshop would look, only plastic. There are so many elves you couldn't count them on your fingers and toes, and of course, there's Santa and his eight glowing reindeer.

Word around the neighborhood is that Mr. Pritchard has to rent a special generator every December just to light up the outdoor decorations. I think it's all pretty exciting.

Every year while Mr. Pritchard is putting up the decorations, Mrs. Pritchard and the three Pritchard kids bake hundreds of Christmas cookies and then invite everyone on the block to join them for hot cocoa and carols on Christmas Eve. But we never go. I don't think anyone in the neighborhood has ever gone. At least, not until tonight.

Tonight started off like most other Christmas Eves. My dad came home early from work and then had to run to the grocery store to pick up something Mom had forgotten to buy for dinner.

When he left, a few snowflakes were beginning to fall. But by the time he got home, it was so snowy, I could barely see out of my bedroom window. Our car got stuck at the bottom of our driveway in a big drift of snow and ice. Then all of the lights started flickering off and on. Our turkey was about half-cooked when the power went out—and stayed out.

Everything was dark. Everything, that is, except for the Pritchard's front yard. The elves kept glowing and the angels kept flapping while all of the neighbors peered out of the windows of their dark houses in amazement.

Five minutes passed. Then ten. It looked like the only thing stirring this Christmas Eve would be the Pritchards.

"I guess we can give up any hope of Christmas dinner," my mom said.

Just then, there was a loud knock at the door. Who do you think was shivering on our front porch in a Santa Claus outfit? You guessed it. Mr. Pritchard...

"We've got lots of Christmas cookies and a freezer full of Valentine's Day cupcakes that are beginning to thaw," he said, smiling a big, toothy grin. "Come on over and we'll bring some of the elves inside so we can read the Christmas story!"

Before my dad could answer, Mr. Pritchard was hurrying across our yard toward the house next door.

"Well, I'll be..." said my dad with a chuckle. He turned to my mom and me and asked, "What do you think? Shall we give the Pritchards a try?"

My mom didn't seem too excited about the idea, but I could hardly wait to see how the Pritchards really celebrated Christmas! I guess the rest of the folks on our block were as curious as I was, because as Mom and Dad and I made our way to the Pritchard's house, it looked like the whole neighborhood was out for a stroll in the blizzard.

"Make yourselves at home," said Mrs. Pritchard as she welcomed us inside. She took everyone's coat and hat and hung them up on the antlers of a large fake moose head in the hall. "I sure hope you're hungry. There are rolls and cranberry sauce in the kitchen, and the turkey should be done any time now."

Sure enough, there in the fireplace was the biggest turkey I had ever seen. The Pritchard kids were all straining together to keep the spit turning and the turkey roasting evenly over the crackling flames.

"We lose a lot of stuffing this way, but it wouldn't be a Pritchard family Christmas without a fireplace-roasted turkey!" said Mrs. Pritchard.

We helped Mrs. Pritchard pass out paper plates and cups of cider, and then we all sat down on the family room carpet as Mr. Pritchard brought in a few plastic elves from outside to light up the room.

Well, we ate and sang by elf-light and laughed until our stomachs were sore. We had so much fun that the whole neighborhood promised we'd be back for New Year's Eve. I just hope this year when Mr. Pritchard drops his "Time's Square ball" off the roof of their house that he misses the cat.

The Three Kings

BY HENRY WADSWORTH LONGFELLOW
ILLUSTRATED BY MARSHA K. HOWE

Three Kings came riding from far away,
　　Melchior and Gaspar and Baltasar;
　Three Wise Men out of the East were they,
And they traveled by night and they slept by day,
　　For their guide was a beautiful, wonderful star.

The star was so beautiful, large and clear,
　　That all the other stars of the sky
Became a white mist in the atmosphere;
And by this they knew that the coming was near
　　Of the Prince foretold in the prophecy.

Three caskets they bore on their saddle-bows,
　　Three caskets of gold with golden keys;
Their robes were of crimson silk, with rows
Of bells and pomegranates and furbelows,
　　Their turbans like blossoming almond-trees.

And so the Three Kings rode into the West,
　　Through the dusk of night over hill and dell,
And sometimes they nodded with beard on breast,
And sometimes talked, as they paused to rest,
　　With the people they met at some wayside well.

"Of the Child that is born," said Baltasar,
　　"Good people, I pray you, tell us the news;
For we in the East have seen His star,
And have ridden fast, and have ridden far,
　　To find and worship the King of Jews."

And the people answered, "You ask in vain;
　　We know of no king but Herod the Great!"
They thought the Wise Men were men insane,
As they spurred their horses across the plain
　　Like riders in haste who cannot wait.

And when they came to Jerusalem,
    Herod the Great, who had heard this thing,
Sent for the Wise Men and questioned them;
And said, "Go down unto Bethlehem,
    And bring me tidings of this new king."

So they rode away, and the star stood still,
    The only one in the gray of morn;
Yes, it stopped, it stood still of its own free will,
Right over Bethlehem on the hill,
    The city of David where Christ was born.

And the Three Kings rode through the gate
    and the guard,
    Through silent street, till their horses turned
And neighed as they entered the great inn-yard;
But the windows were closed, and the doors
    were barred,
    And only a light in the stable burned.

And cradled there in the scented hay,
    In air made sweet by the breath of kine,
The little Child in the manger lay,
The Child that would be King one day
    Of a kingdom not human, but divine.

His mother, Mary of Nazareth,
    Sat watching beside his place of rest,
Watching the even flow of his breath,
For the joy of life and the terror of death
    Were mingled together in her breast.

They laid their offerings at his feet:
    The gold was their tribute to a King:
The frankincense, with its odor sweet,
Was the Priest, the Paraclete;
    The myrrh for the body's burying.

And the mother wondered and bowed her head,
    And sat as still as a statue of stone;
Her heart was troubled yet comforted,
Remembering what the angel had said
    Of endless reign and of David's throne.

Then the Kings rode out of the city gate,
    With a clatter of hoofs in proud array;
But they went not back to Herod the Great,
For they knew his malice and feared his hate,
    And returned to their homes by another way.

A Christmas Tree

BY CHARLES DICKENS
ILLUSTRATED BY MARK DIXON

I have been looking on, this evening, at a merry company of children assembled round that pretty German toy, a Christmas Tree. The tree was planted in the middle of a great round table, and towered high above their heads. It was brilliantly lighted by a multitude of little tapers; and everywhere sparkled and glittered with bright objects. There were rosy-cheeked dolls, hiding behind the green leaves; and there were real watches (with movable hands, at least, and an endless capacity of being wound up) dangling from innumerable twigs; there were French-polished tables, chairs, bedsteads, wardrobes, eight-day clocks, and various other articles of domestic furniture among the boughs, as if in preparation for some fairy housekeeping; there were jolly, broad-faced little men, much more agreeable in appearance than many real men—and no wonder, for their heads took off, and showed them to be full of sugar-plums; there were fiddles and drums; there were tambourines, books, work-boxes, paintboxes, sweetmeat boxes, peep-show boxes, and all kinds of boxes; there were trinkets for the elder girls, far brighter than any grown-up gold and jewels; there were baskets and pin-cushions in all devices; there were guns, swords, and banners; there were gypsies standing in enchanted rings of pasteboard, to tell fortunes; there were tee-totums, humming-tops, needle-cases, pen-wipers, smelling-bottles, conversation-cards, bouquet-holders; real fruit, made artificially dazzling with gold leaf; imitation apples, pears, and walnuts, crammed with surprises; in short, as a pretty child, before me, delightedly whispered to another pretty child, her bosom friend, "There was everything, and more."

The Wonderful Birthday Star

BY ANDREA DORAY • ILLUSTRATED BY LINDA CURELL

Once upon a time, there was a happy mouse family. They lived in a little straw house in the back of a stable. There was a mouse mother and a mouse father and lots of mouse brothers and sisters.

Melissa Mouse was the youngest mouse in the family. She was a big help to the family because she went with her brothers and sisters to gather grain and oats for food, and she helped keep their straw house clean.

But Melissa had a problem. She was afraid to sleep in the dark.

So every night, Mother Mouse would leave a little candle burning in Melissa's room to help her fall asleep. If Melissa woke up, she would see the light and not be afraid.

Father Mouse would always tell stories to the family before bedtime. One of Melissa's favorite stories was about a wonderful birthday from a long time ago. It was the story of the very first Christmas.

Melissa often asked Father Mouse to tell the story of that wonderful birthday.

"It was in a stable just like ours," said Father Mouse, "that the miracle of the first Christmas took place. When Joseph and Mary arrived in the town of Bethlehem after a long journey, there was no place for them to stay."

"But," said Father Mouse, "the innkeeper said they could sleep in the stable, because Mary was going to have a baby. All the animals in the stable shared their home with Joseph and Mary, and, during the night, the baby Jesus was born! A very large and bright star came to shine over the stable to mark the birth of the Son of God."

"Why did the star shine so brightly?" asked Melissa.

"Many people wanted to come see the baby Jesus," said Father Mouse. "The star helped show the way to the stable. And all the people who saw the star knew something wonderful had happened, and they were glad."

Every time Father Mouse would tell this story, Melissa wondered about the bright and shining star that marked the birthday of the baby Jesus.

One Christmas Eve, the mouse family gathered around Father Mouse to hear the story of the first Christmas before they all went to bed.

While the rest of the mouse family was still asleep, Melissa Mouse woke up. The candle in her room had gone out!

At first, she was very afraid. She started to call for Mother and Father Mouse, but then she noticed a bright light shining outside the little straw house.

"What can that be?" asked Melissa. Then she remembered it was Christmas Eve. Could this be the bright and shining star that marked the birthday of the Son of God?

Melissa got up from her bed and went to the window. There were many stars in the sky, but one of them was especially bright. Suddenly, as Melissa watched this bright star, she wasn't afraid anymore. She began to understand why the people wanted to find the stable where the baby Jesus was born. They wanted to be near the Son of God. And she knew why the people were glad when they saw the bright and shining star on the first Christmas.

"Because of the baby Jesus," she said, "there will always be light in the world! It will never be dark because of the shining star that marks His wonderful birthday!"

Melissa went to her bed and fell asleep, even though there was no candle to light her room. When Mother Mouse came to wake her up on Christmas morning, she saw the candle had burned out.

"Were you afraid?" asked Mother Mouse.

"I saw the wonderful birthday star and I wasn't afraid," said Melissa. "But I wish the birthday star could shine all the time."

"The birthday star does shine all the time," said Mother Mouse. "It shines in your heart when you think about the baby Jesus, and it shines for all the world to see when you are happy."

The mouse family celebrated Christmas with a marvelous dinner. They gathered around the table and told each other about things that made them happy.

"I'm happy that we have a warm house to keep us safe and dry," said Mother Mouse.

"I'm happy that we have our family," said Father Mouse.

"I'm happy that we have good food to eat!" said her Biggest-Brother Mouse.

"And I'm happy that it's Christmas!" said Melissa Mouse. "Thank you, Baby Jesus, for the wonderful birthday star!"

Santa Takes a Snooze

BY NAN ROLOFF
ILLUSTRATED BY YUDTHANA PONGMEE

Have you have heard about the Christmas Eve when Santa Claus was just too tired to make his rounds? Here's what happened! He decided to test one of those new-fangled, hand-held video games. Well, he did so well on Level One, he just had to try Level Two, and Three, and on and on 'til before he knew it, he'd been at it for hours and hours!

His eyes hurt, his neck was stiff, and his fingers kept jabbing at the air! He was so exhausted, he kept nodding-off the whole time the elves and Mrs. Claus were loading up the sleigh.

Now usually in this kind of story, some elf or snowman or whatever comes to the rescue. Let's get real! Who do you think bails out Santa when he gets in a tight spot? The Mrs., of course! So Mrs. Claus called an emergency meeting of the elves and reindeer team.

"This calls for drastic action!" announced Mrs. Claus.

"What are we gonna do? He can't keep his eyes open for five minutes!" moaned Elrod, the head elf.

"I'll just have to do the deliveries myself," Mrs. Claus decided.

"But do you know the way?" asked the head reindeer. "I can remember part of it, but, gee, I don't know…"

"How hard can it be? I'm sure I can figure it out. But let's bundle up Santa and put him in the back seat just in case. We'll wake him up if we get desperate."

"What will the kids think? What if they see you?" chorused the team.

"No problem! I'll just put on one of his extra suits. I can make myself a beard out of some teddy bear plush."

"You think of everything!" Elrod admitted with genuine admiration.

Soon Mrs. Claus was comfortably suited up (a pillow stuffed in front) with her long white braid peeking ever so slightly from beneath her red Santa hat. Santa was happily snoring away in the back seat, his favorite bear nestled in his arms.

Up they leapt into the sky, through the Milky Way, over the Big Dipper, and past the North Star. Around the world they flew, past sleepy mountain villages and foggy fishing towns, deep into the dark night.

Snuggling under her comforter, little Jenny Bell had a few questions for her mother.

"Santa's a boy, right?"

"Yes, dear," answered her mother.

"And are all the elves boys?" Jenny frowned.

"Ah, well…I guess they are." Jenny's little frown deepened.

"And I suppose the head of the reindeer team, the one with the red nose—he's a boy, too?"

"Yes, I think so…"

"And Frosty—the snowMAN?"

"Honey, is there a point to all these questions?"

"What's the deal here, Mom? How come they're all boys?" Jenny folded her arms.

"Now, sweetie, I'm sure some of the reindeer are girls and there must be some girl elves," soothed her mom.

"No, the elves all have little beards and wear those little trousers and…"

"Sweetheart, let's just enjoy Christmas and not worry about it, okay? I mean, we don't know for a fact about any of this. Grownups can only guess."

So with a kiss goodnight, Jenny settled into a deep, if not totally contented, sleep while overhead, Mr. and Mrs. Claus were getting lost.

Santa suddenly sat upright and started giving his beloved wife some advice.

"Don't turn so sharp. Don't hold the reins so tight! Aren't you flying a little low?"

Mrs. Claus smiled patiently at her mate. "Why don't you just go back to sleep, dear? I've been doing just FINE."

"Watch that star! Slow down! Where are we?"

"We've got one more stop in the woods around here. A little girl named Jenny Bell. Actually, I need to know exactly where her house is."

"H-m-m-m…"

"Well?"

"I know it's close. Let's see. Maybe…" Santa scratched his head.

"Let's stop and ask directions." The elves jumped for cover behind the toy sack.

"What?! No way! I'm Santa! And Santa doesn't ask directions!"

"Then where's the turn?"

"Right here. No, wait. Keep going. Stop! No, maybe…"

And that's how Santa's sleigh just happened to touch down at an all-night gas station in Newton, U.S.A., much to the surprise of Harold Bartholomew Potter, who had generously volunteered to man the pumps on Christmas Eve because he was feeling grouchy and cynical about Christmas.

"Young man," said Mrs. Claus, in her stuffed suit, "could you direct me to the Bell residence?"

He couldn't believe his eyes! Two Santas! One taking notes, the other waving rather sheepishly from the backseat of a—yes—it was a real sleigh! He just couldn't believe it. He drew the first Santa a map.

"Thank you so much, young man. Here, you look bored. Have a tin of butter cookies and this new hand-held video 'Game Dude'—puhlease, take it!"

"Awesome! Wow! Thank you and, and—Merry Christmas!" Harold B. Potter would never be cynical about Christmas again.

"Merry Christmas!" Santa and Mrs. Claus and the elves all shouted. And they were gone in a twinkling.

Jenny stirred as she heard the light tapping on the roof. Santa? "Oh, oh—too exciting!" She listened—barely breathing. Oh, for a chance to see him! "Oh, please, oh, please," Jenny whispered as she tiptoed down the hall. "I forgive you for having all boy elves and a boy head reindeer and…"

There he was, standing in the soft glow of the Christmas lights, gently placing Jenny's gifts beneath the tree.

It was Santa Claus! Santa Claus? Jenny rubbed her eyes. What was that peeking out from under his hat? It looked like a braid, just like Grandma Louisa's. Then "Santa" turned and pulled down his beard to scratch his chin, spotted Jenny, and gave her a wink. Whoa! Jenny ran back to bed as fast as she could and dove under the covers. "So much to think about…" she mused as she dozed off to sleep.

As for Santa and the Mrs., they got home just fine. They made some hot chocolate and settled down in their easy chairs to discuss how things went.

"Well, I guess you did okay," Santa offered.

Mrs. Claus raised an eyebrow.

"Actually, you did great. In fact, I kinda like having you along. Maybe we should make a habit of this," Santa chuckled.

"Thank you very much. I just might take you up on that," smiled Mrs. Claus.

After giving each other a big hug, they exchanged gifts. Santa got a pair of heated foot massagers and Mrs. Santa got an expresso maker. And then they both settled down for a long winter's nap.